Da Vinci

Wendy Conklin, M.A.

Consultants

Timothy Rasinski, Ph.D.
Kent State University

Lori Oczkus, M.A.
Literacy Consultant

Publishing Credits

Rachelle Cracchiolo, M.S.Ed., *Publisher*
Conni Medina, M.A.Ed., *Managing Editor*
Dona Herweck Rice, *Series Developer*
Emily R. Smith, M.A.Ed., *Content Director*
Stephanie Bernard/Susan Daddis, M.A.Ed., *Editors*
Robin Erickson, *Senior Graphic Designer*

The TIME logo is a registered trademark of TIME Inc.
Used under license.

Image Credits: Cover, pp.1, 21 North Wind Picture Archives; back cover and p.4 Heritage Image Partnership Ltd/Alamy Stock Photo; p.7 Mondadori Portfolio/Getty Images; p.11 Fine Art Images/Heritage Images/Getty Images; pp.13, 14 Bridgeman Images; p.17 The Print Collector/Getty Images; pp.18–19 Art Media/Print Collector/Getty Imagesl p.20 Apic/Getty Images; p.22 PAINTING/Alamy Stock Photo; p.27 vkstudio/Alamy Stock Photo; all other images from iStock and/or Shutterstock.

Library of Congress Cataloging-in-Publication Data

Names: Conklin, Wendy, author.
Title: 16th century superstar : Da Vinci / Wendy Conklin, M.A.
Description: Huntington Beach : Teacher Created Materials, 2017. | Includes
  index.
Identifiers: LCCN 2016037450 (print) | LCCN 2016038325 (ebook) | ISBN
  9781493836307 (pbk.) | ISBN 9781480757349 (eBook)
Subjects: LCSH: Leonardo, da Vinci, 1452-1519--Juvenile literature. |
  Artists--Italy--Biography--Juvenile literature. |
  Scientists--Italy--Biography--Juvenile literature.
Classification: LCC N6923.L33 C66 2017 (print) | LCC N6923.L33
(ebook) | DDC
  709.2 [B] --dc23
LC record available at https://lccn.loc.gov/2016037450

Teacher Created Materials

5301 Oceanus Drive
Huntington Beach, CA 92649-1030
http://www.tcmpub.com

ISBN 978-1-4938-3630-7

Table of Contents

A Superstar Is Born

Every now and then, a superstar comes along and the world takes notice. By definition, superstars stand out. This is certainly true of Leonardo da Vinci. He was born in Vinci, Italy, in 1452. Had his mother not been a peasant, things might have turned out differently for da Vinci. He most likely would have attended the university in Florence and studied to be a **notary** like his well-to-do father. Instead of painting and inventing ways to solve problems, his days would have been busy filling out legal documents.

But his parents never married. So the **guild** of the magistrates and notaries would not accept da Vinci as an **apprentice**. Instead, his father had to look for another profession for him. As a young child, da Vinci showed a talent for drawing. So his father sent him to Florence to become an apprentice to the famous artist, Andrea del Verrocchio. And that is where the road to superstardom began for da Vinci.

Da Vinci was continually striving to improve and perfect his work and the world around him. Along the path to becoming a superstar, da Vinci came into contact with many different types of people. They played important roles in his life as he developed not only as an artist but also as a scientist and inventor.

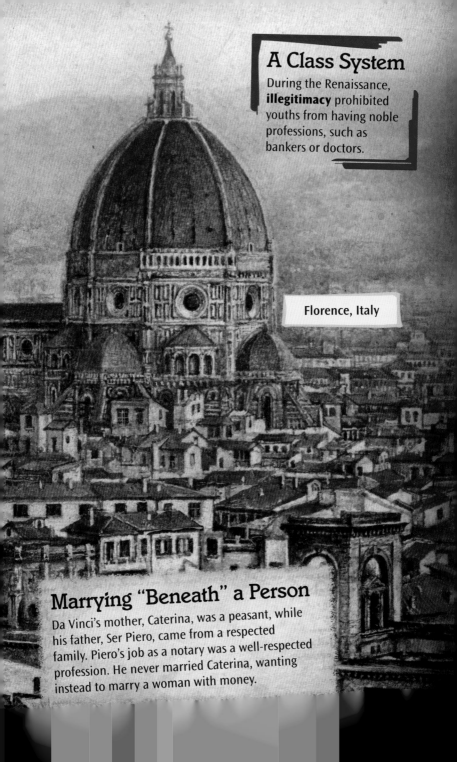

A Class System

During the Renaissance, **illegitimacy** prohibited youths from having noble professions, such as bankers or doctors.

Florence, Italy

Marrying "Beneath" a Person

Da Vinci's mother, Caterina, was a peasant, while his father, Ser Piero, came from a respected family. Piero's job as a notary was a well-respected profession. He never married Caterina, wanting instead to marry a woman with money.

A Superior Apprentice

From the very beginning, da Vinci stood out in Andrea del Verrocchio's workshop. Even though he was an illegitimate child, he was one of the wealthiest apprentices at the workshop. He came from his father's "respectable" family. This was rare for Verrocchio's apprentices in 1467. Most boys came from homes where the fathers were typical **tradesmen**.

Verrocchio designed sets and costumes for pageants. The artists in his workshop painted banners, carpets, and **tapestries** for festivals. **Patrons** often commissioned paintings. And, everyone worked together. As the master painter and sculptor, Verrocchio directed the work.

Students were craftsmen. They learned by practicing their master's style of artistry. This made it all the more remarkable when da Vinci began practicing his own painting techniques. Da Vinci's skills are obvious in the 1475 work *Baptism of Christ*. The monks of San Salvi near Florence commissioned this painting. Verrocchio asked da Vinci to paint the angel on the far left. The result amazed everyone. Da Vinci's style stands out as superior. Verrocchio realized that his student, at just 23 years old, had surpassed him.

Not a Finisher

Throughout his life, many of da Vinci's paintings and projects went unfinished. There are different theories as to why. Some investigations reveal that he had such varied interests that is was difficult for him to complete one task before moving on to the next. Other historians believe he left works unfinished because he was a perfectionist. If his work could not achieve perfection, he abandoned it.

A Man without Education

When asked, da Vinci described himself as *"omo sanza lettere."* This means that he was a man without an education. The local priests taught him to read, write, and solve basic arithmetic, but that was the extent of his formal education.

Baptism of Christ

How to Paint like Leonardo

Some artists today still follow da Vinci's process. Here are the steps they take to create masterpieces and experience the rewards of creating works of art.

1. Artists sketch and plan the composition that will become the painting. This can take months to complete.

2. They make the **cartoon**, which is the finished sketch of the painting. It will be as large as the painting, so they might connect several papers together to make it as large as it needs to be.

3. Next, they attach the cartoon to a wall or other spot where the final painting will be located.

4. Following the outlines of the cartoon, artists poke small holes in the paper.

5. Pressing chalk into the holes transfers the chalk onto the wall. When they remove the cartoon from the wall, it leaves the outline of the painting.

6. Artists then lay the **underpainting** by using neutral earth tones. These tones create the shadows that give the painting a three-dimensional look.

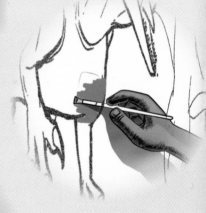

7. Finally, they add the color to the painting by applying layers of oil paints until the painting is complete.

Seeking a Patron

In 1482, da Vinci was commissioned by the ruler of Florence to create a silver *lyra de braccio*. The instrument, shaped like a horse's skull, was a gift to Ludovico Sforza. He was the duke of Milan. Da Vinci delivered it himself and caught Sforza's attention with his skill in playing the *lyra* and singing.

Not too long afterward, da Vinci wrote the duke a letter explaining that he was looking for a new patron. He stated that his knowledge and imagination could benefit Sforza. Remarkably, working as a musician was not mentioned. Instead, da Vinci listed his ideas for a range of war machines and innovative battle tactics. He had ideas for drying up water in moats during a siege. He also proposed digging tunnels under rivers so that armies could advance against foes. If these ideas were not enough he could work as an architect, a sculptor, or even a painter.

Da Vinci knew about Sforza's reputation as a man of war and used it to his advantage. While he was waiting for an answer from Sforza, he earned a commission from the monks at the Church of San Francesco Grande.

A Man of Peace

In spite of his many ideas for warfare, da Vinci was known as a man of peace. His reputation was one of harmony and calm. In fact, he isn't known to have had any fights with other people.

A Covered Car

Da Vinci sketched many ideas in his notebooks. This includes an idea for a covered car that could attack an enemy in battle. His vision became reality about 430 years later in the form of a tank.

THINK LINK

- What traits made da Vinci stand out from other apprentices in Verrocchio's studio?
- How do da Vinci's actions to become a part of Sforza's **court** show that he was a strategic person?
- Why do you think da Vinci left out the part about his skills as a musician?

The Church of San Francesco Grande needed an altarpiece. So in 1483, da Vinci was hired and given strict instructions. The contract stated that he would create a painting that included Mary, Jesus, angels with halos, and two prophets. The painting would show God looking down from above wearing gold and blue. It also stated the pay would be 800 *lira*, with a bonus to be determined by the monks. Da Vinci signed the contract, but surprisingly, he did not follow it.

Instead, he painted baby Jesus sitting in the grass, completely unclothed, along with the infant St. John. He depicted Mary as a young girl and only included one angel, instead of several. The most scandalous thing of all is that no one had a halo. That had never been done before. And he completely omitted God and the two prophets! The painting became known as the *Virgin of the Rocks*.

Da Vinci and his two assistants asked for more money once the painting was completed. The monks stuck to the original agreement instead of giving da Vinci what he wanted.

Lifelike Portraits

Before da Vinci's time, emotions and realism were not shown in paintings. Most subjects held blank stares and did not elicit feelings from the viewer. In his sketches and portraits, da Vinci explored ways to portray his subjects more realistically. One of his famous portraits, *The Lady with the Ermine*, shows both the woman and the animal with very detailed features.

STOP! THINK...

- In what ways did da Vinci stray from the contract on his *Virgin of the Rocks* painting?
- How would adding the monks' requirements change the painting's mood?
- Why do you think da Vinci ignored the monks' requirements regarding the painting?

Virgin of the Rocks

After viewing the breathtaking *Virgin of the Rocks*, Ludovico Sforza was convinced that da Vinci's various talents would benefit his court. The duke called upon him to create a heating system for the duchess's bath. Da Vinci also engineered canals in Milan and designed military weapons and forts. When a special event or pageant was held, da Vinci planned all the details, including choosing music and designing costumes. At a gala, da Vinci produced the stage set for the *Feast of Paradise* performance. This showed actors dressed as the planets rotating in the sky. The back lighting made them look like actual stars.

Sforza commissioned da Vinci to paint *The Last Supper* on the back wall of the Santa Maria della Grazie in Milan. He pressured da Vinci to complete it quickly. But da Vinci was not one to hurry his work. Even the **prior** wouldn't leave him alone. The story goes that an irritated da Vinci threatened to use the prior's face for Judas, the **betrayer** of Christ, in the painting. After that, da Vinci was not bothered again. Da Vinci was one of the first to include Judas among Christ's 12 **disciples**. This was a very daring move for the artist.

The Last Supper Did Not Last

Da Vinci did not want to paint *The Last Supper* as a **fresco** because he wanted to take his time while painting, and watercolors on plaster would not allow for that. He also wanted the painting to be more detailed and radiant. So instead, he used a mixture of oil and tempera paints, which unfortunately faded because of the humidity in the monastery.

More Than a Painter

When the bubonic plague began killing thousands of people, da Vinci devised a plan to rebuild Milan. He believed that his new city plan, which would house 30,000 people, could prevent an outbreak. His plan included dividing the city into 10 districts on the Ticino River. They would then redistribute the population to avoid high-density areas. Each district would connect to the next by roads and canals. This would allow for more access to water for cleaning and transportation. The streets would have two tiers. The lower tier would be for the wagons, animals, and working people's homes. The upper tier would be for pedestrians and the homes of the wealthy. Da Vinci believed that this separation of the classes would prevent the rampant spread of the plague.

Da Vinci had many personal interests as well, such as understanding the human body. Although it was against the law, da Vinci dissected corpses. This wasn't just to understand how to draw the body. He also wanted to know how the organs worked. He recorded all his findings in notebooks.

Everywhere he went, da Vinci carried a miniature notebook with him in his belt. His notebooks contained jokes, philosophical thoughts, sketches of buildings, maps, and plans for his paintings. Since he was able to write with both hands, he sometimes wrote backwards with his left hand because it was more convenient.

The Notebooks

Instead of writing whatever came into his mind, da Vinci organized his notebooks in a systematic way. Entire sections of notebooks would be about **anatomy**, mechanics, painting, and so on. Some historians say he was inspired by colleagues who were publishing volumes of books on single topics, such as architecture.

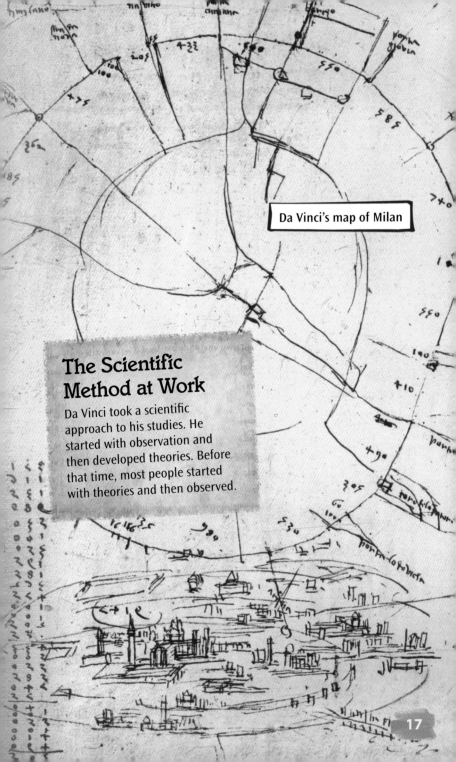

Da Vinci's map of Milan

The Scientific Method at Work

Da Vinci took a scientific approach to his studies. He started with observation and then developed theories. Before that time, most people started with theories and then observed.

Shortly after da Vinci arrived in Milan, he began work on a bronze statue of a horse. It was to be dedicated to the duke's late father and former duke, Francesco Sforza. For years, da Vinci planned the sculpture by making countless drawings in his notebooks. He decided to make the sculpture four times larger than life size. This was something that had never been done before.

After 12 years, da Vinci presented a full-size clay model of the sculpture, standing 24 feet (7.32 meters) tall. Da Vinci knew he had to invent a method for **casting** the bronze on such a large piece. If the molten bronze cooled too quickly, it would crack. So, he determined that four different furnaces would enable him to do it successfully.

When he was finally ready to cast the statue, the necessary 70 tons (63,502 kilograms) of bronze were ordered. Unfortunately, before work on the sculpture could begin, that bronze had to be used to make cannons. The French had threatened Milan, and the city needed to be ready for battle.

The bronze statue was never cast. When the French captured Milan in 1499, they used the magnificent clay model as target practice and completely destroyed it.

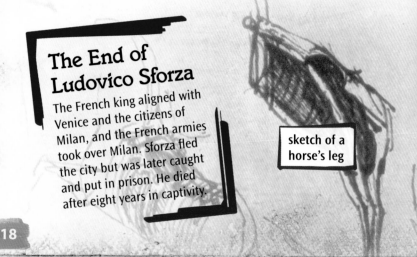

The End of Ludovico Sforza

The French king aligned with Venice and the citizens of Milan, and the French armies took over Milan. Sforza fled the city but was later caught and put in prison. He died after eight years in captivity.

sketch of a horse's leg

When da Vinci illustrated in his notebooks, he wrote words to clarify the illustrations. Before this time, illustrations were used in books to clarify the writing. Today, modern scientific illustrations use the same technique as da Vinci did.

bronze horse drawing
from da Vinci's notebooks

Military Engineer and Architect

Da Vinci fled to Venice in late 1499, after the French conquered Milan. The *Signoria* was the governing body in Venice. They asked him for some military advice. There was cause to be worried. Turkish warships filled the waters around the city, and soldiers camped nearby on land.

He got to work sketching devices that would enable the Venetian army to operate underwater. Da Vinci believed that if the army could get to the Turkish ships and drill holes in them, the ships would sink. Then, the enemy could be defeated.

He designed an underwater breathing tube and deep-sea diving suit. With that, the Venetian troops could advance through the water unseen. He also proposed special shoe attachments that could allow Venice's soldiers to walk on water. Unfortunately, da Vinci only stayed in Venice a few months and none of his designs were actually built.

The First Idea for a Submarine

Da Vinci also created ideas for what is known today as a submarine. Even though none of his proposed ideas were actually used in Venice, his notebooks show these designs in great detail.

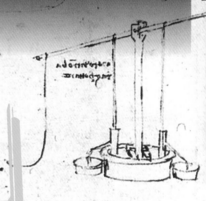

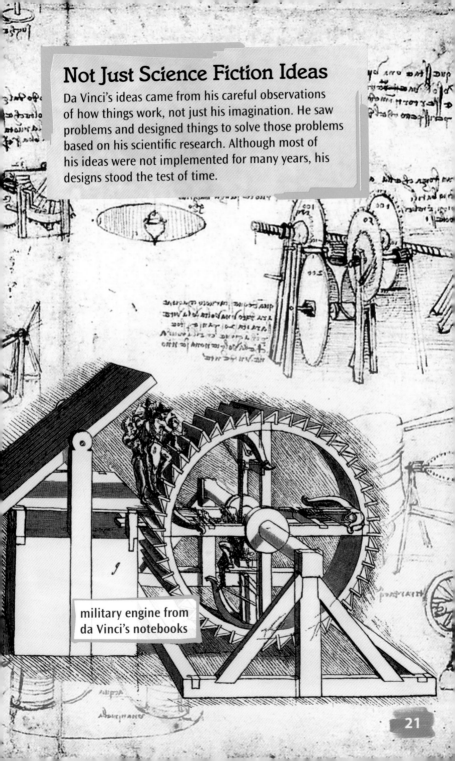

Not Just Science Fiction Ideas

Da Vinci's ideas came from his careful observations of how things work, not just his imagination. He saw problems and designed things to solve those problems based on his scientific research. Although most of his ideas were not implemented for many years, his designs stood the test of time.

military engine from da Vinci's notebooks

By 1502, da Vinci was working for Cesare Borgia in Rome. There, he served on a committee researching architectural issues of the church of San Francesco al Monte. Borgia hired him as his engineer and senior military architect. At first, da Vinci did not mind Borgia's reputation as a brutal military leader. Da Vinci wanted the chance to travel and practice his skills.

Diverting Rivers as Military Strategy

After da Vinci left Rome, he went to Florence to help the city, which was in a power struggle with Pisa. He devised plans to divert the Arno River so that Pisa's water supply would be cut off. His strategy was not a success.

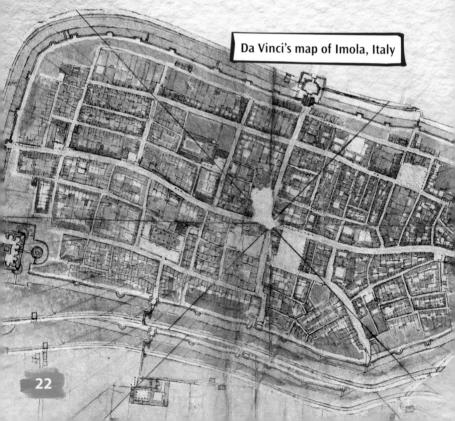

Da Vinci's map of Imola, Italy

Meeting Machiavelli

During his travels, da Vinci met the writer Niccolò Machiavelli. Machiavelli's most famous book was *The Prince*, which was based on Borgia. It discussed how to be a ruthless leader.

Borgia's father, Pope Alexander VI, was a powerful man. Borgia used the papal armies to conquer most of central Italy. Someone needed to survey the land to see how much land had been captured. Da Vinci sketched **meticulous** maps of the areas where he traveled. His bird's-eye view of Imola, Italy, was one of the first of its kind.

He also worked as Borgia's military engineer and architect. He oversaw construction of fortresses and inspected them. He drew several sketches of weapons to be used in battle as well.

But all good things must come to an end. After just ten months, da Vinci felt some of Borgia's war tactics were too vicious, so he left.

An Infamous Portrait

Da Vinci went back to Florence in 1503. He began painting his most famous work, the portrait known as the *Mona Lisa*. Many art historians have speculated that this painting depicts Lisa Giocondo, who was the wife of the wealthy Francesco del Giocondo. Rumor had it that Francesco commissioned this painting in celebration of his new home and the birth of his first son.

Da Vinci knew anatomy better than anyone at the time, so he could accurately paint the various parts of the face. Instead of painting in profile, he turned the subject two-thirds toward the viewer. This allowed him to use different techniques. Other artists would soon begin to imitate his style.

He used **sfumato** to blur lines into each other. You can see this technique on the robe and smile in the painting. He also used the technique of **chiaroscuro**, which means to play with light and shadow. This made the woman's hands appear three-dimensional.

The portrait took years to complete, but he didn't deliver it. Instead, he kept it with him for the rest of his life.

Da Vinci's Skill

Other artists watched da Vinci apply his unique techniques as he painted the *Mona Lisa*. They often tried to copy these techniques, but no one could match his skill. After the *Mona Lisa*, artists began painting more realistic work. Examples include Raphael's paintings *The Alba Madonna* and *The Transfiguration*.

Other Ideas about Mona Lisa's Identity

Some scholars and historians believe that the *Mona Lisa* was Giuliano de' Medici's mistress. Others say it was a self-portrait of da Vinci or a boy dressed as a woman. These researchers and art experts are still searching for a definitive answer behind that mysterious smile.

Mona Lisa

Final Days

Da Vinci went to France just a few years before he died. He had spent the last couple of years in Rome, but when his patron, Giuliano de' Medici, died, King Francis I summoned him. Da Vinci was given the title of First Painter, Architect, and Engineer. He was over 60 years old at this time, but the king felt it was only right to make da Vinci's last years both comfortable and peaceful. He lived in a chateau and was visited frequently by the king. At only 20 years old, the king wanted to learn from da Vinci, who had so much knowledge.

While in France, da Vinci finished his exquisite painting titled *St. John the Baptist*. This masterpiece proved to be very different from others on the same subject. Instead of painting St. John as a rugged man, da Vinci depicted him with a feminine face. He also spent time planning various building projects, as he was painting very little by this time. Instead, he was busily organizing the thousands of pages in his notebooks. On May 2, 1519, Leonardo da Vinci quietly passed away.

Da Vinci's legacy lives on in his art, writing, and sketches. He was a lifelong learner, and his uniqueness helped to shape how the world sees him today.

The Myth of da Vinci's Death

It's not certain if King Francis I really held da Vinci in his arms when he died, but it is a commonly told story. King Francis I wanted people to think that he was with da Vinci at the end.

Scientist and Artist

At the time da Vinci died, he was known primarily for his artwork. Years later, his notebooks gave new insight into his thinking as a scientist. He believed that art and science were intertwined.

St. John the Baptist

Glossary

anatomy—the structure of humans, animals, and plants

apprentice—a young person who works for someone else to learn a trade

betrayer—someone who is unfaithful to another person to hurt that person

cartoon—the finishing sketch that artists use as a guide before painting a scene

casting—putting liquid metal in a mold to form it

chiaroscuro—the art of distributing light and shade in a picture

court—group of people who assist an important person

disciples—followers

fresco—painting on moist plaster

guild—an organization of people in the same industry or interest

illegitimacy—being born of parents who are not married

lyra de braccio—Renaissance stringed instrument of the violin family

meticulous—very careful or exact

notary—someone who prepares contracts and legal documents

patrons—people who pay artists to pursue their skills or crafts

prior—the monk ranked just below the head of a monastery

sfumato—the blurring of lines in a painting

tapestries—pictures or designs made from woven threads on fabric

tradesmen—people who are skilled at a certain craft

underpainting—first coat of paint on a canvas that acts as a base

Index

Check It Out!

Books

Augarde, Steve. 2009. *Leonardo da Vinci.* Kingfisher.

Grey, Christopher. 2008. *Leonardo's Shadow: Or, My Astonishing Life as Leonardo da Vinci's Servant.* Atheneum Books for Young Readers.

Napoli, Donna Jo. 2009. *The Smile.* Speak.

Romei, Francesca, Sergio Ricciardi, and Andrea Ricciardi. 2001. *Masters of Art: Leonardo da Vinci: Artist, Inventor and Scientist of the Renaissance.* Peter Bedrick Books.

Ross, Stewart. 2004. *Leonardo da Vinci: Scientists Who Made History.* Hodder Wayland.

Videos

Renato Castellani. *The Life of Leonardo da Vinci.* Questar.

Luciano Emmer and Enrico Gras. *Genius—Leonardo da Vinci.* Cromwell Productions.

Websites

History Channel. *Leonardo da Vinci.* http://www.history.com/topics/leonardo-da-vinci/videos.

Museum of Science. *Leonardo da Vinci: Scientist, Inventor, Artist.* http://legacy.mos.org/leonardo/.

Try It!

Just like da Vinci, you are an inventor. Look back through the reader at all the ideas he sketched and wrote. He developed many of them to solve a problem or to help people.

- Think about all the places you go and people you come into contact with every day. Observe your surroundings.

- What is something you could invent to help a parent, a teacher, a peer, an animal, or a business?

- Sketch some ideas in a notebook (like da Vinci did). Label the parts of your invention diagram and how they will work.

- Name your invention. Write a paragraph with the diagram that explains whom it will help and how.

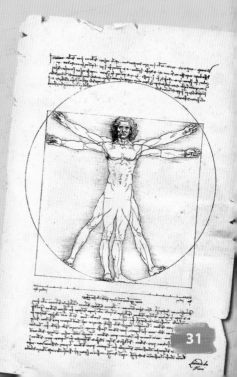

- If you have materials available, build a model of your invention to go with the sketch and paragraph.

About the Author

Wendy Conklin has spent the last 15 years honing her skills as a writer for both teachers and students. She is always looking for ways to be creative in both her writing and in the things she chooses to do in her everyday life. She lives with the belief that the secret to being creative is to put oneself in situations to learn new skills, and so now she spends much of her time learning upholstering, drawing, and playing the guitar. Her next endeavor will be photography!